Persecution and Emigration

David Downing

WORLD ALMANAC® LIBRARY

Please visit our web site at: www.worldalmanaclibrary.com
For a free color catalog describing World Almanac® Library's list of
high-quality books and multimedia programs, call 1-800-848-2928 (USA)
or 1-800-387-3178 (Canada). World Almanac® Library's fax: (414) 332-3567.

Library of Congress Cataloging-in-Publication Data

Downing, David, 1946-
    Persecution and emigration / by David Downing.
        p. cm. — (World Almanac Library of the Holocaust)
    Includes bibliographical references and index.
    ISBN 0-8368-5944-8 (lib. bdg.)
    ISBN 0-8368-5951-0 (softcover)
    1. Jews—Persecutions—Germany—Juvenile literature. 2. Holocaust, Jewish (1939-1945)—
Germany—Juvenile literature. 3. Refugees, Jewish—Europe—History—20th century—
Juvenile literature. 4. Germany—Social conditions—1933-1945—Juvenile literature.
5. Germany—Ethnic relations—Juvenile literature. I. Title. II. Series.
DS135.G3315.D68   2005
940.53'18—dc22   2005042113

First published in 2006 by
World Almanac® Library
A Member of the WRC Media Family of Companies
330 West Olive Street, Suite 100
Milwaukee, WI 53212 USA

Copyright © 2006 by World Almanac® Library.

Produced by Discovery Books
Editors: Geoff Barker, Sabrina Crewe, and Jacqueline Gorman
Designer and page production: Sabine Beaupré
Photo researchers: Geoff Barker and Rachel Tisdale
Maps: Stefan Chabluk
Consultant: Ronald M. Smelser, Professor of Modern German History, University of Utah
World Almanac® Library editorial direction: Mark J. Sachner
World Almanac® Library editor: Alan Wachtel
World Almanac® Library art direction: Tammy West
World Almanac® Library production: Jessica Morris

Photo credits: cover: USHMM, courtesy of National Archives; title page: Keystone/Getty Images;
p. 5: National Archives/Newsmakers/Getty Images; p. 6: Mary Evans Picture Library/Weimar Archive;
p. 8: Mary Evans Picture Library; p. 9: Topfoto.co.uk; p. 10: Topfoto.co.uk; p. 11: Topfoto.co.uk; p. 13:
Topfoto.co.uk; p. 14: Topfoto.co.uk; p. 17: Mary Evans Picture Library; p. 19: Keystone Features/
Getty Images; p. 21: Bettmann/CORBIS; p. 22: Mary Evans Picture Library; p. 25: Mary Evans Picture
Library; p. 27: Bettmann/CORBIS; p. 28: Mary Evans Picture Library/Weimar Archive; p. 31: Mary
Evans Picture Library; p. 32: Keystone/Getty Images; p. 34: Keystone/Getty Images; p. 36: Mary Evans
Picture Library/Weimar Archive; p. 40: Fred Morley/Fox Photos/Getty Images; p. 41: Three Lions/Getty
Images; p. 43: Topfoto.co.uk.

Printed in Canada

1 2 3 4 5 6 7 8 9 09 08 07 06 05

Cover: The window of a Jewish-owned store was broken during *Kristallnacht*, a night of
violent action against Jews in Germany in November 1938.

Title page: In 1938, the Nazis decided to expel all Polish-born Jews in Germany. Thousands of
people became refugees when Poland refused to let them in. These refugees, stuck at Zbonszyn
on the Polish-German border, had nowhere to go.

Contents

The Holocaust

The Murder of Millions

The word *holocaust* has a long history. In early times, it meant a burnt offering to the gods, and in the **Middle Ages**, a huge sacrifice or destruction. It still has this second meaning today, particularly when used to describe large-scale destruction by fire or nuclear weapons. But since the 1970s, the word has gained a new and specific meaning. Today, when people refer to the Holocaust—with a capital "H"—they mean the murder of approximately six million Jews by Nazi Germany and its **allies** during World War II.

This crime had deep historical roots. In predominantly Christian Europe, the Jews had always been considered a race apart and had often endured persecution for that reason. When governments or peoples wanted someone to blame for misfortune, they often picked on an innocent and helpless, Jewish minority.

In the early twentieth century, many Germans wanted some-one to blame for their defeat in World War I and the terrible economic hardship that followed. They, too, picked on the Jews in their midst—with ultimately horrific results. The Holocaust was ordered and organized by political leaders, carried out by thousands of their willing supporters, and allowed to happen by millions of ordinary people.

The scale of the crime is still hard to take in. To use a modern comparison, about three thousand people were killed in the **terrorist** attacks in the United States on September 11, 2001. Between June 1941 and March 1945, an average of four thousand European Jews were murdered every day.

These people were killed in a variety of ways. Some were left to starve, some to freeze. Many were worked to death in **labor camps**. More than one million were shot and buried in mass graves. Several million were gassed to death in specially built **extermination camps** such as Auschwitz and Treblinka.

The Persecution of the Jews

Jews were not the only victims of the Nazis. In fact, it is probable that the Nazis and their allies murdered at least five million other **civilians** before and during World War II. Their victims were killed for a variety of reasons: **communists** for their political opinions, **homosexuals** for their sexual orientation, people with mental disabilities for their supposed uselessness to society, **Gypsies** and Slavs for their supposed racial inferiority, and Russians, Poles, and other eastern Europeans because they happened to be in the Nazis' way.

The central crime in the Holocaust—the murder of millions of Jews—was a long time in the making. Most of the actual killing took place between 1941 and 1945, but the Jews of Germany were subject to intense persecution from the moment Adolf Hitler and his Nazi Party took power in 1933. That persecution was itself merely the latest in a series of persecutions stretching back over almost two thousand years, in which every nation of Europe had at some time played a part.

This book looks at the period between the Nazis taking power in 1933 and the outbreak of World War II in 1939. For German Jews, these were years of persecution, fear, and dread.

The Dachau concentration camp was liberated by the U.S. Seventh Army on April 29, 1945. Clothing belonging to prisoners was piled up high—slave laborers had been forced to strip before they were killed.

CHAPTER ONE

Nazi Anti-Semitism

A Long History

The phrase **anti-Semitism**, meaning racial prejudice against Jews, is not much more than one hundred years old. But the prejudice itself—mostly in religious form—stretches back over approximately two thousand years of European history. From the moment that Christianity became the dominant religious force in European life, Jews were forced into the role of a minority. When things went wrong—a plague, a bad crop, an economic crisis—the reaction of many was to blame the Jews.

Things improved from the eighteenth century on, as political and economic developments, together with new attitudes to individual freedoms, made religious differences less important. Many Jews, particularly in western Europe and North America, were tolerated in businesses and professions from which they had previously been barred. Small but vocal groups of anti-Semites remained in most of these countries, however, and in

Joseph Goebbels, Adolf Hitler's propaganda chief, was fiercely anti-Semitic. He is pictured here in Berlin in 1931.

the 1920s, several German groups sought popular support by falsely blaming the Jews for their country's defeat in World War I (1914–1918) and the economic setbacks in the following decades. The most successful of these scapegoaters were Adolf Hitler and his Nazi Party.

Hitler and the Nazis

According to Hitler and the Nazis, the Jews were not real Germans. Instead, they belonged to a different race. This distinction was crucially important. The Jewish people had been considered members of many groups over the previous two thousand years—members of a religious group, of a cultural group, of a nation, of a race—but membership in the first three had become increasingly a matter of choice. In twentieth-century western Europe, Jews could choose not to believe in **Judaism**, to live however they wanted, and to promise their loyalty to whichever nation they lived in. Jews could be **citizens** like everyone else.

The Nazis refused to accept any of this. They didn't care what Jews believed, how they lived, or which nation they claimed as their own. In the Nazis' view, the Jews were a race apart, and they could never be anything else.

The Nazi Creed

"Why do we oppose the Jews?

"We are enemies of the Jews because we are fighters for the freedom of the German people. The Jew is the cause and the beneficiary of our misery. He has used the social difficulties of the broad masses of our people to deepen the political divisions among our people. He has made two halves of Germany. He is the real cause for the loss of the Great War.

"The Jew is responsible for our misery and he lives on it. That is the reason why we oppose the Jew. He has corrupted our race, fouled our morals, undermined our customs, and broken our power."

Joseph Goebbels, Nazi Party propaganda chief, in an article called "Why Do We Hate The Jews?"(1930)

CHAPTER TWO

Setting the Jews Apart

The Jews in Germany

In the two national elections of 1932, the Nazis won more seats in the *Reichstag* (the German parliament) than any other party, and, in January 1933, their leader Adolf Hitler was appointed **chancellor**. At this time, there were around half a million Jews living in Germany, or slightly less than 1 percent of the population. In general, they neither lived nor worked separately from non-Jewish Germans. Jews worked in the legal and medical professions, owned businesses, and were prominent in the arts and media. Many were married to non-Jews. Jews were an integral part of German society, much as they were, for example, integral parts of French or American societies.

The Nazis set out to reverse this state of affairs. They wanted to set the Jewish community apart from the rest of Germany in every way that they could—economically, culturally, and physically.

In Berlin in April 1933, German "patriots" discourage people from buying goods at Jewish stores.

Books that were seen as "un-German" were burned on the Opera Square, Berlin, in May 1933. This incident provoked a wave of disgust throughout the world.

The First Two Years

The economic campaign began with a one-day **boycott** of Jewish businesses on April 1, 1933. The word *Jude* (Jew) and the Star of David (the best-known symbol of Judaism) were painted on shop and café windows, and **stormtroopers** stood outside holding signs and threatening violence against anyone trying to enter. Days later, new laws were introduced that prohibited Jews from working for the state as civil servants or teachers. Over the next few months, similar action was taken against Jewish lawyers, doctors, dentists, publishers, and others. Jews were also forbidden to own farmland.

Similar measures were introduced in the nation's cultural life. Jewish actors and musicians were forbidden to perform, and books written by Jews were burned in public ceremonies across Germany. The German Jewish poet Heinrich Heine (1797–1856) was one author whose works were fed to the flames. A century earlier, he had written, prophetically, that "those who begin by burning books end by burning people."

Increasing efforts were made to separate the Jews physically from the rest of the population. They were forbidden entry to swimming pools and many parks and forced to use separate

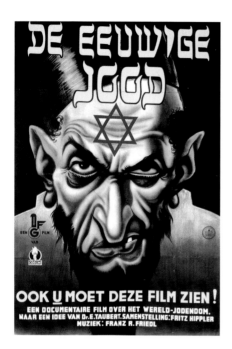

This Dutch poster for the anti-Semitic film *De Eeuwige Jood* (*The Eternal Jew*) demonstrates the level of anti-Jewish feeling in the 1930s.

seating areas in those places that still admitted them. In their eagerness to show their Nazi credentials, café proprietors, shop owners, and even whole villages put up signs denying entry to Jews and proudly proclaiming themselves *Judenfrei* (free of Jews).

Propaganda and Violence

The stream of anti-Jewish laws was reinforced by ferocious propaganda and the constant threat, and frequent use, of physical violence. Nazi films, radio programs, and newspapers never tired of criticizing, ridiculing, or pouring scorn on what they called "the Jew" (as if Jews were things rather than human beings). The weekly Nazi newspaper *Der Stürmer* contained an endless stream of bloodthirsty anti-Semitic rants. And since no anti-Nazi media were allowed, Germans never heard the opposing view.

Most important of all, anti-Semitism was taught in all non-Jewish schools. The new textbooks, covering all subjects, were full of anti-Semitic slurs and lies. Jewish writers were banished from literature and Jewish scientists from science. In Nazi Germany, history was being rewritten as a tale of German greatness and Jewish betrayals.

Perhaps above all else was the violence. Any German Jew who walked down the street knew that he or she was running the risk of being beaten. In March 1933, the British newspaper the *Manchester Guardian* reported many such beatings, "until the blood streamed down their heads and faces, and their backs and shoulders were bruised. Many fainted and were left lying on the streets." A few Jews were even killed. It was no use going to the police. As far as the police and their Nazi masters were concerned, the law existed to protect "real Germans"—not Jews.

The Reaction of Non-Jewish Germans

How did ordinary non-Jewish Germans react to this rising tide of violent anti-Semitism? Some were opposed—with reactions ranging from thorough disgust to mere disapproval—but few

Julius Streicher and *Der Stürmer*

The weekly newspaper *Der Stürmer* was established by the Nazis in 1923 and edited for many years by Julius Streicher, a close friend of Hitler. When the Nazis came to power, Streicher was given the province of Franconia to rule. He became notorious for his cruelty and the fact that he always carried a whip. On one occasion, he had 250 Jewish tradesmen arrested and then ordered them to mow a field with their teeth.

Der Stürmer was violently anti-Semitic and often almost pornographic. The slogan "The Jews are our misfortune" appeared under the title on each front page. One special issue, in May 1934, was devoted to reviving the "blood libel" against the Jews, an old claim that Jews used the blood of Christian children to make matzo, the special bread used on the holiday of Passover. Issues of *Der Stürmer* could be read in display cases on the streets of German cities. The display cases were removed in 1936, when the Summer Olympic Games were held in Berlin, to avoid upsetting visiting foreigners. The display cases were put back once the Olympics were over. *Der Stürmer* was said to be the only publication that Hitler read from cover to cover.

Teaching Racial Prejudice

"The first important lesson to be learned was how to spot a Jew. For a time, Jewish children were still allowed to attend school, and they were used as specimens, standing before the class, while the teacher pointed out certain racial characteristics: shape of nose, shape and size of head, set of eyes, skin color and so on. Particular attention was paid to the low forehead, long skull, short, weakling physique and the fact that Jewish boys were circumcised. For contrast and to emphasize the lesson, pure Nordic and Germanic types also stood up in front of the class to be analyzed. Their characteristics, classes were told, made them a 'chosen race' created in the image of God to possess power, knowledge, culture, and the talent for organization. This instruction was backed up in the textbooks, one of which had a chapter titled 'Characteristic and Distinguishing Features of Jews' and photographs of Jews, in profile and full-face like prisoners in custody, hung on the walls."

Brenda Ralph Lewis, from the book Hitler Youth *(2000)*

people said so. They knew that if they spoke out, they risked being beaten themselves or, far worse, being given a one-way ticket to a **concentration camp**.

Many other Germans were pleased to see the Jews in such trouble. Some really believed the anti-Semitic propaganda, while others saw opportunities for their own advancement. They took the jobs of Jews who had been fired and snapped up the houses and businesses that Jews were forced to sell at rock-bottom prices.

Most ordinary non-Jewish Germans did nothing. They wanted to believe their government's propaganda because the alternative— opposing the government— was too dangerous and frightening to think about. They looked at conditions in Germany. They saw that unemployment figures were beginning to fall, and they told themselves that if Hitler was right about the economy, then he might be right about the Jews, as well. They received no moral guidance from the Catholic Church, which agreed not to criticize the Nazis if the Nazis left it alone, or from the Protestant churches, most of which supported the regime. A few brave church figures, including Pastor Martin Niemoller and Bishop Clemens von Galen, spoke out against the Nazis' treatment of Jews, but most Christian leaders remained silent.

A Promise and a Threat

Other groups were also persecuted during the early years of the Nazi regime. The first occupants of the new concentration camps were political opponents, mostly communists and **socialists**. Some of these people were Jewish, but that was not the reason they had been arrested. In July 1933, the Law for the Prevention of Offspring with Hereditary Diseases, which legalized the forced **sterilization** of many people suffering from either mental or physical disabilities, was introduced. In later years, it would be extended to legalize their murder.

The sign in Schwedt, on the River Oder, reads "Jews not wanted in this place!" These posters were put up in sites all over Germany beginning in July 1935.

Everyone knew, however, whom the Nazis hated most. By the summer of 1935, Jews were banned from military service, one in three German Jews had lost their jobs, and two centuries of the Jews' gradual **integration** into German society had been reversed. The Jews, Nazi propaganda chief Joseph Goebbels promised in 1934, would be left alone "as long as they retire quietly and modestly behind their four walls, as long as they are not provocative, and do not affront the German people with the claim to be treated as equals."

CHAPTER THREE

The Nuremberg Laws and "Aryanization"

The Nuremberg Laws

By the autumn of 1935, Germany's Jews had been set apart from their non-Jewish neighbors and forced to accept a vastly inferior status. Neither non-Jewish Germans nor the international community had come to the aid of Germany's Jews in any significant way. Encouraged by this lack of opposition to its anti-Semitism, the Nazi government increased its persecution of the Jews. The aim of the Nuremberg Laws, which were introduced in September 1935, was to make the separation of German Jews and non-Jews permanent and deny Jews those rights that non-Jews took for granted.

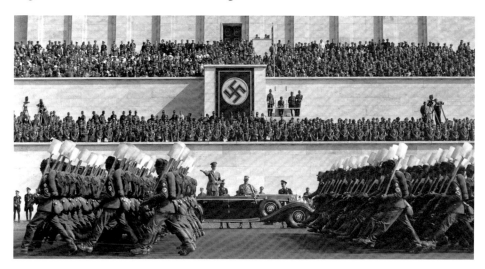

The Nuremberg Rally was a huge show of strength by the Nazi Party. It took place every year from 1933 to 1938, in Nuremberg, Germany. The rallies included parades that marched past Nazi leader Adolf Hitler, such as this one held in September 1935.

In order to persecute the Jews, Nazis first had to define who they counted as a Jew. The Nazi Party would have liked to include anyone with "Jewish blood," but this would have meant tracing family histories back hundreds of years and would probably have led to millions of Germans—and some Nazi leaders—being defined as Jewish. Instead, a compromise was reached. According to the Nuremberg Laws, anyone with three Jewish grandparents was a Jew, but a certain amount of confusion remained about those with one or two Jewish grandparents. To reduce this problem in the future, Jews and non-Jews were forbidden to marry or have sexual relations with each other.

There was no doubt, however, about the status of those who were defined as Jews. They were stripped of their German **citizenship,** as Hitler had promised as far back as 1920 (when the Nazi Party had issued a program outlining its plans). The Nuremberg Laws turned the Jews into "subjects" of the state, people without rights or the protection of the law.

The Nazi Definition of a Jew

The Reich Citizenship Law of 1935, part of the Nuremberg Laws, defined who was to be counted as a Jew:

1. A Jew is a person descended from at least three Jewish grandparents who are full Jews by race.

2. A subject of the State of mixed descent . . . who is descended from two full Jewish grandparents is also considered a Jew if: (a) he belonged to the Jewish religious community at the time this law was issued or joined the community later; (b) he was married to a Jew at the time the law was issued, or if he married a Jew subsequently; (c) he is the offspring of a marriage with a Jew, which was contracted after the Law for the Protection of German Blood and Honor went into effect; or (d) he is the offspring of extra-marital intercourse with a Jew and will be born out of wedlock after 31 July, 1936.

"Aryanization"

Foreign opinion about the Nuremberg Laws was mostly hostile. The *Herald Tribune*, a U.S. paper, reported the new laws under the headline "The Shame of Nuremberg," and the London *Times* thought their "complete disinheritance and **segregation** of Jewish citizens" was a throwback to "medieval times." Rather than risk a foreign boycott of the 1936 Summer Olympic Games, scheduled to be held in Berlin, the Nazi government turned down the volume of its anti-Semitism during

The Berlin Olympics

The Nazis wanted the 1936 Olympic Games in Berlin to be a good advertisement for their regime. As a result, signs saying "Jews not welcome" were removed from hundreds of shops, hotels, and restaurants. The German Olympic team even included part-Jewish competitors. Some German Jews saw this fact, and the sudden downplaying of anti-Semitism during the Olympics, as signs that the worst was over. They were mistaken. Just 10 miles (16 kilometers) from the Olympic stadium, at Sachsenhausen, a concentration camp was being built.

The 1936 Olympics are often remembered for the fact that an African American, Jesse Owens, won four gold medals and made a mockery of the idea of a German "master race." However, Germany did win more gold, silver, and bronze medals than any other nation, and many Nazis felt this justified their sense of superiority.

Interestingly, two Jewish sprinters—Marty Glickman and Sam Stoller—were removed from the U.S. 4x100 yard relay team at the last minute. The U.S. Olympic authorities claimed that they had simply picked better runners, but both Avery Brundage, the chairman of the U.S. Olympic Committee, and Dean Cromwell, the assistant track coach, were known Nazi sympathizers. The suspicion remains that it was anti-Semitism that cost Glickman and Stoller their places on the relay team.

This Jewish shop in Berlin was defaced with the word *Jude* (meaning Jew) as part of the Nazi campaign of boycotting Jewish business.

the first half of 1936. Nothing had really changed, however. Once the Olympics were over and the foreigners had gone home, the Nazis stepped up their efforts to make economic life difficult for the Jews. Between 1933 and 1935, the government had already removed all Jews from government jobs and from professions such as law and medicine. Now, they concentrated on driving them out of the business world, starting with the largest and most visible businesses—publishing companies, banks, and big department stores. Jewish owners and managers were forced out and replaced by non-Jews. This process was officially known as Aryanization, but it was really just a form of theft. Now that they were mere "subjects" of the German state, the Jews had no legal defenses and nothing with which to bargain. They had no choice but to take whatever they were offered for their businesses, which was rarely more than a fraction of what their enterprises were worth.

Jews who had managed to remain in business through the first four years of Nazi rule had often helped to support those family members and friends who lost their jobs. Fewer and fewer were now able to offer such help, and the Jewish community as a whole was rapidly sliding into poverty. New taxes on Jewish "wealth" made the situation still worse. By the end of 1937, Germany's Jews had not only been set apart but also, in large measure, deprived of the freedom to earn a living.

CHAPTER FOUR

Jewish Options

As 1937 gave way to 1938, the situation of Germany's Jews continued to worsen. What options did they still have? Essentially, they had three. They could try to fight back, they could try to leave Germany, or they could simply sit tight and hope for the best.

Drawing Closer Together

It was a hopeless task to fight back with the goal of reversing the Nazis' anti-Jewish policies. The policies were driven by anti-Semitism, not by reason, and rational protests or discussions were meaningless tools against such prejudice. Jews were not allowed to publish writings or speak on the radio, and so they had no way to appeal to the non-Jewish German public. Even if they had, and even if that public had been willing to listen, there was no way to force a change in Nazi government policy. There were no elections and no **democratic** institutions. In addition, any Jew who spoke out was almost certain to be badly beaten and sent to a concentration camp without having a trial.

Fighting back in the physical sense was likely to result in imprisonment or death. The Jews were a small, largely defenseless minority; the Nazi German state was defended by well-armed men with military experience and, in many cases, a taste for violence.

If active resistance was impossible, Jewish cultural life, at least, remained alive. German Jews became more self-reliant. Because their children could not go to ordinary German schools, Jews ran their own. Because their musicians could not play in public halls, they gave private concerts. Jewish religious festivals became more important as Germany's Jews drew closer together, and **synagogue** attendance grew. For the first

The synagogue in Danzig (now Gdansk) was burned out by the Nazis in November 1938 during their push for control of the Polish city. One banner reads, "The synagogue is to be demolished." Another adapts the lyrics of a well-known song of the time, "Come, beloved May, and make the trees green," to "Come, beloved May, and make us free from the Jews."

five years of Nazi rule, German Jews struggled, against all odds, to make the best of the separate society that the Nazis had forced them to become.

The Difficulties of Emigration

Between 1933 and 1938, about one-fourth of German Jews left Germany to live elsewhere. They were driven to make this move by insult, humiliation, random violence, state-sanctioned robbery and murder, and general denial of their right to make a living. At first glance, their decision to leave seems much more understandable than the decision made by the other 75 percent of German Jews to stay. Why did those men and women decide against **emigration**, in many cases until it was too late to go?

Emigration is never easy. It is always hard to leave one's own country and set off for another with little or no money, little or no knowledge of the language, and no home or job to which to go. Leaving Germany immediately after the **Great Depression** began (in 1929) was even harder, especially because the Nazi government would not allow Jews to take more than a tiny fraction of their belongings with them.

People also needed documents to emigrate. Before World War I, traveling between countries had been a reasonably simple matter, but the huge movements of population that followed the war persuaded governments to make it much more difficult

Pride of the Persecuted

Some German Jews saw Nazi persecution as an opportunity to take pride in their Jewishness. In April 1933, after the Nazi boycott of Jewish stores, one Jewish newspaper editor, Robert Weltsch, noted that the Stars of David painted on the Jewish-owned shops had been "meant to dishonor us." On the contrary, he said, "Jews, take it upon yourselves, that Star of David, and honor it anew."

Increasingly, as the Nazi years went by, German Jews were forced to provide for each other what the state refused to provide, and this created a new sense of solidarity and unity in their community. The Central Organization of German Jews (which, in 1935, was forced to change its name to the Central Organization of Jews in Germany) established a secret university and organized new colleges to teach trades and agricultural skills. Young Jews realized that they had no professional future in Germany and that having a trade would help their chances of being taken in by another country. They flocked to locally organized courses in cooking, tailoring, woodworking, and other occupational skills.

Many children were among the Jewish refugees who fled Germany. These children were making a temporary home at a British summer resort in Dovercourt, England, in 1938. They would then find temporary shelter with British families before moving on again.

to cross borders. Governments began insisting that people carry passports or visas, which were formal documents issued by the government. Despite their stated desire to be rid of the Jews, the Nazi authorities made it difficult for Jews to get hold of the documents they needed.

After World War I, most governments had also begun to limit the number of **immigrants** they were prepared to accept, and the growth of unemployment that accompanied the Great Depression led to further reductions. If there weren't enough jobs for their own workers, governments argued, then they could hardly take in more, especially the now-impoverished German Jews. Each Jew wishing to leave Germany had to find a place in a foreign government's **quota**, or number of people allowed to enter for a particular year. If the quota was already filled, then people wishing to emigrate had to wait for the next year or try another country whose quota might not be filled.

By early 1938, it was clear that there were simply not enough places in the world's quotas for all the Jews who wanted to leave Germany. In July 1938, a conference was held in Evian, France, to discuss the situation. Thirty-two governments sent representatives, but only three of them—the Netherlands, Denmark, and the Dominican Republic—agreed to increase the number of Jewish immigrants they would accept. The majority followed the lead of the United States and Britain, both of which rejected any increase.

Palestine

Jewish immigration to one particular land, however, was a special case. During World War I, the Ottoman Turks had been driven out of Palestine—the land now divided between Israel and the Palestinian National Authority—by the British. In 1917, the British foreign secretary, Arthur Balfour, had announced that his government favored the creation of a national home-land in Palestine for the Jewish people. After the war, Britain was given the job of administering Palestine, and part of this job included setting quotas for Jewish immigration.

Some German Jews emigrated to Palestine before the Nazi era. This photograph of the Ben-Schemen colony dates from about 1905.

Unfortunately for Germany's Jews, the Arabs in Palestine, who made up a majority of the population, had become alarmed by the rise of the Jewish population there during the 1920s and the first half of the 1930s. By the late 1930s, when German Jews most needed entry, the British could not expand the quota without provoking an explosion of Arab anger. In addition, Palestine was rarely the first choice of German Jews hoping to emigrate. It was still a poor and—to the average western European—undeveloped country, offering few of the comforts that most Europeans took for granted. It would turn out, however, to be a much safer haven than countries such as Denmark and the Netherlands, which would soon find themselves occupied by Germany.

Reasons to Stay

The German and other governments put formidable obstacles in the way of German-Jewish emigration, but there was also a reluctance to leave on the part of Jews themselves. Put simply,

World Jewry

In 1937–1938, the total number of Jews worldwide was probably between 15 and 17 million, of whom about 5 million lived in the United States and Canada. Another 1 million lived in western Europe, including the 350,000 or so still in Germany, and just under 0.5 million in Palestine. The greatest concentration of all—some 7 million Jews—lived in a vast area of eastern Europe often called "the Pale (meaning territory) of Settlement." This region included most of Poland and much of western Russia and the Ukraine, and it stretched south into Romania and north into Lithuania. Another 2–3 million Jews were scattered throughout most of the remaining countries of the world.

Mixed Signals

"I was hiking in the mountains with a group of friends, having a glorious time. We found a farmhouse where people took overnight guests, and decided to spend the night. The woman invited us to come in, and offered to show us the room. It was a nice room, but on the wall hung pictures of Hitler. I immediately told her, 'I'm sorry we have bothered you. We are Jews.'

" 'Oh, please come in,' she said. 'It's all our fault. The situation during the Depression was very bad. Hitler promised that he would make many changes, and so we voted for him. Now you can't even open your mouth; if you criticize something you get in trouble for it.'

"While she was talking this way she suddenly said, 'Here comes Elizabeth, our daughter. She is fourteen years old, and I cannot say in front of her what I said to you. I have to be quiet because she would tell her Hitler Youth leader everything I said and we would be in serious trouble.' "

From the self-published memoirs of Martha Pappenheim,
who left Germany early in 1939

they were not at all sure that life would be better elsewhere. Today, looking back at the horrific things that happened to Europe's Jews, such a view seems almost incredible. But at the time, it was not an unreasonable view to hold.

On the one hand, fewer than two hundred Jews had actually been killed in Nazi Germany by the end of 1937. The Jewish community had been treated atrociously, but it was still alive. There was no hint as yet of mass murder. On the other hand, conditions for Jews were not necessarily favorable elsewhere because anti-Semitism was clearly alive and well around the

Polish Jews were angered by the repression and prejudice they had to endure. This demonstration in April 1933 took place in Lodz, Poland.

world. The Jews of Germany were well aware of Russia's anti-Semitic history, for example, since many of their ancestors had come from there in past centuries. In more recent years, anti-Semitic activity in Poland, Romania, and Hungary had grown alarmingly as their governments and peoples followed Germany's example. In Palestine, Jews were being murdered by Arabs; in the United States, they were being targeted by racist groups such as the Ku Klux Klan.

Given all this, and given the difficulties involved in emigration and the fear of jumping from an anti-Semitic frying pan into an anti-Semitic fire, it is not surprising that many German Jews chose the third option: to sit tight and hope for the best. They hung on to their homes and the streets they knew and chose to believe that all bad things would eventually come to an end. They told themselves that things had to get better. They had no way of knowing that things were about to get much, much worse.

CHAPTER FIVE

Nazi Intentions

One reason that most German Jews chose to stay in Germany, at least until the winter of 1938–1939, was their uncertainty over Nazi intentions. Until 1938, the Nazis did not make those intentions clear. Sometimes they issued bloodcurdling threats of annihilation, but at other times, they indicated that Jews would be allowed to live a peaceful, separate existence.

Did the Nazis themselves know in early 1938 what they intended? It is clear that their policies were driven by hatred of the Jews, but it is not so clear what those polices actually were at the beginning. Some historians believe the Nazis always meant to kill as many Jews as they could and simply waited for the opportunity to do so. Most historians, however, reject the idea of a master plan, arguing that the Nazis responded to changes in circumstance. They say that the Nazis considered the Jews a "problem" and came up with a series of "solutions," none of which proved completely successful. It was only later, about 1941, that the Nazis decided on their "final solution": the killing of all Jews.

Contradictory Policies

From 1933 to 1937, during the first years of the **Third Reich**, the Nazis followed two, often contradictory, policies. They tried to set Jews apart in a separate, inferior nation inside Germany. At the same time, though, they tried to persuade the Jews to leave. In one sense, these policies worked together. German Jews were more likely to try to emigrate if their lives were made miserable inside Germany. In practice, however, these policies contradicted each other. The more the Nazis impoverished the Jews, the more reluctant other nations were to accept them.

After the Evian Conference in 1938, where the world's nations refused to increase significantly the number of Jews they would

The Evian Conference at Evian les Bains, France, in July 1938 discussed the problem of political refugees. Lord Winterton, leader of the British delegation, is seen here addressing the conference of thirty nations.

accept, Adolf Hitler mockingly said that he would put Jews aboard "luxury ships" if that would help get rid of them. He didn't mean it. In reality, his government continued to make it difficult for Jews to leave. To emigrate, Jews needed many different documents and had to surrender almost all their possessions. If the Nazis had really wanted to make Germany *Judenfrei*, they could have given Jews the documents, offered them proper compensation for their assets, and allowed them to leave with what money they had. Then other nations would probably have been more willing to take in Jewish immigrants.

A Desire to Hurt

Why did the Nazis behave in this contradictory manner? There is one obvious explanation: Nazis took pleasure in hurting Jews. However much they liked the idea of getting rid of Jews, they liked the idea of depriving Jews of their wealth, dignity, and freedom even more.

This hunger for revenge against the Jews—revenge for crimes that were wholly imaginary—infected Nazi policy from top to bottom. Hitler was the main driving force, but his rage

Palästin

Bild-Beil
der Jüdischen Rundsc
Berlin W 15, Meinekestraß

Nr. 5 99 vom 12. Dezember

Chanukah-Tage im jüdischen

This supplement magazine to the Polish-Jewish *Rundschau*, from December 1933, was promoting Palestine as a suitable destination for Jews.

against the Jews was shared by most members of his party. When Joseph Goebbels said in 1934 that the Jews would be left alone if they were not provocative, he was either fooling himself or simply lying. As far as Hitler and the Nazis were concerned, the Jews' mere existence was a provocation. There was no way on Earth that Jews would be left alone, even as a permanent underclass.

The Nazis' changing views about Jewish emigration to Palestine gives an excellent insight into their attitudes. At first, they liked the idea of sending Jews off to their own national **ghetto** in the Middle Eastern desert. In fact, the Nazis made a deal with the World **Zionist** Congress allowing German Jews to emigrate to Palestine on favorable terms. By the end of the 1930s, however, the Nazis decided that Jews were doing too well there and might create a power base. It would be better, Nazi policymakers said in 1939, if Jews were scattered around the world in other people's countries, so that everyone could learn to hate them as much as the Germans did.

More Territory Brings More Jews

The most important reason for the Nazi failure to rid Germany of its Jews was geographical. The Treaty of Versailles—an agreement between the Allies and Germany after World War I—

The Nazis' Policy on Palestine

During the early 1930s, the British government was prepared to allow a German-Jewish emigrant into Palestine in exchange for a payment of £1,000 (approximately $4,500 at the time). The Nazi government, eager to rid itself of as many Jews as possible, made the Ha'avara Agreement (*Ha'avara* means "transfer" in Hebrew) with the Zionist leadership to enable Jewish emigrants to meet the required payment in a way that benefited the German economy. German Jews sold their assets in Germany and put the proceeds into German banks. The banks used the money to buy German-manufactured goods and ship them to the Jewish-owned Ha'avara company in Palestine. The company sold the goods and gave the proceeds to the emigrants, who could then make the immigration payment. This arrangement appeared to work for all parties and increased the flow of Jews from Germany to Palestine. By the end of 1937, Jews formed almost 30 percent of Palestine's population. A Jewish state seemed the inevitable outcome, and this prospect soon began to worry the Nazis. In January 1939, a government "Memorandum on the Jewish Question" set out the reasons why:

"At first the emigration of German Jews to Palestine received extensive support from Germany through the conclusion of [the Ha'avara Agreement]. . . . But Germany has to recognize the danger in the creation of a Jewish state. . . . The realization that Jewry will always be the implacable enemy of the Third Reich forces us to the decision to prevent any strengthening of the Jewish position. A Jewish state would give world Jewry increased power. . . . Germany has an important interest in seeing the splintering of Jewry maintained. . . . The influx of Jews arouses the resistance of native populations in all parts of the world, and thus provides the best propaganda for Germany's policy towards the Jews. . . . [W]herever the stream of Jewish migrants has poured in, a clear increase in anti-Semitism has already been recorded. It must be the aim of German foreign policy to strengthen this wave of anti-Semitism."

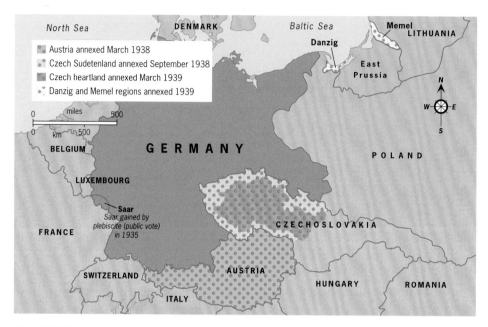

Legend on map:
- Austria annexed March 1938
- Czech Sudetenland annexed September 1938
- Czech heartland annexed March 1939
- Danzig and Memel regions annexed 1939

Saar
Saar gained by
plebiscite (public vote)
in 1935

Adolf Hitler wanted to expand Germany's territories. This map shows the neighboring countries and areas he successfully took over prior to the beginning of World War II, in September 1939.

changed boundaries in Europe. Under the treaty, parts of the German nation were placed within the borders of other nations. Germany and Austria were still populated almost exclusively by Germans; in addition, Czechoslovakia, Poland, France, and Lithuania now contained significant German minorities.

Hitler had long wanted to gather all Germans into one nation, and he intended to do this by redrawing the borders of Central Europe once again. By 1938, after several years of **rearmament**, Hitler felt Germany was strong enough to challenge the existing European order. Austria was his first target. In March 1938, he used the twin threats of a Nazi uprising and a military invasion to bully the Austrian government into accepting the *Anschluss*, the union of Germany and Austria. Six months later, Hitler threatened to invade Czechoslovakia if it did not surrender its German-populated areas, the so-called Sudetenland. At first, the Czechs stood firm, but they were persuaded by Britain and France to give in to German demands at a conference in Munich in September 1938.

Adolf Hitler drives through Vienna in triumph during the annexation of Austria in March 1938.

In the first five years of Nazi rule, about 130,000 Jews had left Germany. The annexation of Austria and the Sudetenland, however, brought in more than twice that number. Far from ridding itself of Jews, Germany was gathering more. If, as seemed likely, Poland was the next target of Hitler's expansionism, another 3 million Jews would be taken into the German fold. Expulsion would no longer be an option.

CHAPTER SIX

The Night of Broken Glass

Dress Rehearsal in Austria

When Austria became part of Hitler's Third Reich in March 1938, all the laws that had been applied to Germany's Jews were applied to Austria's 200,000 Jews as well. Overnight, they lost their citizenship, their right to protection under the law, their choice of work, and their freedom of movement. During the first days of the *Anschluss*, they were also subject to widespread humiliation and cruelty. Jewish men and women were ordered to scrub sidewalks, eat grass, and clean unflushed toilets in front of jeering non-Jewish spectators. In one Vienna

Nazi soldiers and party members look on as Jews are forced to scrub clean the sidewalks of Vienna, Austria.

amusement park, some older Jews were driven at high speed on the park's scenic railroad until several of them suffered heart attacks. Many Jewish men were arrested, taken off to concentration camps, and beaten to death. At least one woman received a parcel containing the ashes of her husband and a bill for his cremation.

This outpouring of **sadistic** behavior, worse than anything so far seen in Germany itself, was condemned by a few news-papers in the Western democracies, but the criticism produced no practical response from their governments. During the Evian Conference of July 1938 (see pages 26–27), most governments refused to increase the number of Jews they were prepared to take in. One month after the meeting, a committee set up by the Evian Conference told the Nazi government that it accepted Germany's right to do whatever it wanted in its own country. If Hitler had needed a green light for stepping up the persecution of Jews inside Germany, he had been given one.

Kristallnacht

The trigger for the "stepping up" was supplied when one Jew decided to fight back. When the Nazis came to power in 1933, the population of Germany included a large number of Polish-born Jews. The Nazis tried to expel them in October 1938, but the Polish government refused to take them back. Thousands ended up trapped at Zbonszyn, on the German-Polish border, without adequate food or shelter. One man, Zindel Grynszpan, wrote to his teenage son Herschel, a student in Paris, France, describing their situation. On November 7, the angry

A Protest to the World

"My heart bleeds when I think of our tragedy and that of the twelve thousand Jews [stranded on the frontier between Germany and Poland]. I have to protest in a way that the whole world hears."

Herschel Grynszpan, writing to his uncle before shooting Ernst vom Rath in the German Embassy in Paris

In November 1938, about 7,000 Polish Jews were expelled from Germany by the Gestapo. Refugees, including children, suffered from exposure as they gathered at Zbonszyn on the Polish-German border.

Herschel went to the German Embassy in Paris and shot the first official he came across, Ernst vom Rath.

The following day, Nazi newspapers reported the shooting and threatened revenge against the Jews. When vom Rath died on November 9, 1938, the order for action was given. That night, a carefully planned tide of stormtrooper violence swept through the German-Jewish community. In town after town, more than 7,000 Jewish-owned shops and warehouses were looted and burned. Almost 300 synagogues were torched and burned to the ground. The broken windows that covered the sidewalks the next day gave the night its name: *Kristallnacht*, the Night of Broken Glass.

The destruction did not stop at property. About 100 Jews were murdered on *Kristallnacht* and more than 30,000 arrested. Of those arrested, about 1,000 were beaten or tortured to death in police stations, **SA** barracks, and concentration camps.

Kristallnacht in Berlin

"I have seen several anti-Jewish outbreaks in Germany during the last five years but never anything as nauseating as this. Racial hatred and hysteria seemed to have taken hold of otherwise decent people. I saw fashionably dressed women clapping their hands and screaming with glee while respectable middle-class mothers held up their babies to see the 'fun.' Women who argued with children who were running away with toys looted from a wrecked shop were spat on and attacked by the mob.

"There were remarkably few policemen on the streets. Those who were, shrugged their shoulders and refused to take any action. Several hundred Jewish shopkeepers were, however, put under 'protective custody' for attempting to shield their property. A state of hopeless panic reigns tonight throughout Jewish circles. Hundreds of Jews have gone into hiding and many businessmen and financial experts of international repute have not dared to sleep in their own homes."

Hugh Carleton Greene, Berlin correspondent of British newspaper the Daily Telegraph, *reporting what he saw on* Kristallnacht *in Berlin, 1938*

The Nazis claimed that *Kristallnacht* had been a spontaneous outpouring of public anger at the murder of vom Rath, and they held the Jewish community responsible for all the damage that the Nazi thugs had done. The German-Jewish community was fined 1 billion Reichsmarks ($400 million)—about one-fifth of all Jewish wealth in Germany—and new anti-Semitic regulations were introduced. The few German-Jewish children who still attended state schools were expelled, and the Gestapo (the political police force) was put in charge of all remaining Jewish organizations.

A Turning Point

Kristallnacht marked a turning point for all Germans. For almost six years, Germany's non-Jewish majority had been fed a regular diet of anti-Semitic propaganda, anti-Semitic laws, and anti-Semitic regulations. Some of them had witnessed violence against Jews on the street. Despite all this, however, most of them were still shocked by the scale and scope of *Kristallnacht*. Many non-Jews told friends and family that they felt ashamed to be German, but what could they do? If they protested, their own lives and families would be at risk. A few people did intervene on behalf of Jews, such as the champion boxer Max Schmeling, who hid Jewish children in his house on *Kristallnacht*. These people often paid for their courage, however, with beatings and imprisonment. The vast majority kept silent. As Deborah Dwork and Robert Jan van Pelt comment in *Holocaust: A History,* their 2003 book on the Holocaust: "The elites did not utter a word. The working class did not utter a word. The middle classes shook their heads in dismay, and said nothing. And thus it was not the Nazis alone who crossed a significant line, but their countrymen too."

For those German Jews who had clung to the hope that Hitler and his Nazis would let them live in some kind of peace,

On November 9, 1938, the Night of Broken Glass, a sickening wave of terror attacks was launched on Jewish stores, on synagogues, and on Jews themselves.

Kristallnacht in Leipzig

"A truck loaded with SA pulled up across the road a few houses down and some twenty young louts jumped down. One carried a clipboard and directed the men to shops and houses in various directions. Some of the stormtroopers rang bells on the opposite side of the road, waited for a reaction, and if this was not forthcoming, smashed the glass windows in the door and bolted up the stairs. In the street, stormtroopers with long steel pikes began smashing shop windows to the loud hooray of their mates. From the houses across the street I could hear screams and yelling, and soon men in heavy coats were being frog-marched down, their clinging wives being peeled off at the door. They were loaded onto the trucks."

Wim van Leer, a young Dutch Jew, describing what he saw on Kristallnacht *in Leipzig, in his book* Time of my Life *(1984)*

Kristallnacht marked the end of the illusion. Those who had recommended emigration had been right all along: Things were only going to get worse. The lines for exit visas and foreign quota places were suddenly five times as long.

What did the rest of the world think about *Kristallnacht*? There were strong words in the world's newspapers and protest demonstrations in the United States. U.S. president Franklin D. Roosevelt temporarily withdrew the U.S. ambassador from Berlin. But no **economic sanctions** were threatened, and no action was taken that would really deter the Nazis from further persecution. As the committee set up by the Evian Conference had said, the German government could do what it liked in its own country. Only one question remained. Now that the threat was so obvious, would the Western powers finally throw their doors open and offer Germany's Jews a place of safety?

CHAPTER SEVEN

Trapped

During the last seven weeks of 1938, most of the 30,000 Jews arrested after *Kristallnacht* were released. As the Nazis had intended, their stories of sadistic beatings and murders increased the desire of their families and friends to leave Germany. Over the winter of 1938–1939, another 120,000 German Jews managed to emigrate, although at the cost of losing almost everything they owned.

The emigrants received help from Jewish and non-Jewish **charity organizations** around the world. These organizations persuaded governments that they would look after Jewish immigrants themselves and make sure that they were not a burden on their new countries. Individuals also helped, and

After Kristallnacht

"Only the employees of the Jewish organizations and some people who rent rooms or cater meals are still earning something. In Berlin, a Jew can get a coffee only in the waiting room of the Zoo Station and a meal in a Chinese or some other foreign restaurant.

"As the Jews are constantly being thrown out of buildings inhabited by 'mixed population' they increasingly move in with each other and brood over their fate. Many of them have not yet recovered from the 9th November [*Kristallnacht*] and are still fleeing from place to place in Germany or hiding in their apartments."

Georg Landauer, the director of the Central Bureau for the Settlement of German Jews in Palestine, describing the situation in Berlin in early 1939

one in particular—Frank Foley, who worked in the British Embassy in Berlin—helped thousands of German Jews to emigrate to Palestine.

Generally speaking, German-Jewish emigrants were scattered across the globe. Large numbers went to North America, South America, South Africa, Australia, Palestine, and Britain. About 20,000 of them ended up in Shanghai, China, because the international settlement in that city was the only destination that did not require a visa. Another 75,000 moved a much shorter distance, into nearby European countries. Most of these Jews would find themselves under Nazi rule again when the German army overran most of the continent between 1939 and 1941, during the first years of World War II.

No Relief

Despite the work of charity organizations and individuals, the number of people wishing to leave Germany was still far more than the number for whom places could be found. The Nazi government wanted its

Frank Foley (1884–1958)

Frank Foley was a British Secret Service (MI6) agent stationed in Berlin during the years of Nazi rule. Officially, he was a passport control officer at the British Embassy, and it was while performing his duties in this position that Foley managed to save thousands of German-Jewish lives. He bent the rules, accepting guarantees of payment that were obviously false and giving out more visas than he was supposed to. He helped Jews get in touch with officials from other embassies who were willing to take bribes. When all else failed, he used his intelligence contacts to help Jews make illegal escapes across the border. Foley remained on the job in Berlin until late August 1939. Years later, German Jews who survived the war dedicated a grove of thousands of trees in his honor near Jerusalem, Israel.

Jewish emigrants to be a burden on their new countries and continued to insist that Jews leave all their wealth and property behind when they left Germany. Governments around the world, fearful of a negative reaction from their own people, continued to restrict the numbers of Jews they would let in.

The U.S. government, for example, decided on admitting a certain number of immigrants per year. There was a list for each year stretching into the future, and German Jews could get themselves on the next list that still had available spaces. Those on the lists for 1939, 1940, and 1941 were all allowed in during 1938 and 1939. It was then decided, however, that people on the list for 1942 would have to wait until that year. If they just let everybody in at once, the U.S. authorities explained, then there was no point in having annual lists.

Helga Samuel, a German-Jewish girl, is met off the boat at Harwich, England, in December 1938. A representative of the *Kindertransports* program examines her identity tag.

The Kindertransports and the St. Louis

After *Kristallnacht* in late 1938, the British government agreed to accept ten thousand German-Jewish children without visas, provided that charity organizations or British families were prepared to take care of them. Over the next few months, trains packed with children left Berlin, Vienna, Leipzig, Frankfurt, Danzig, and other German and Austrian cities for the voyage to Britain.

40

The SS *St. Louis* docked in Antwerp, Belgium, in June 1939. Her cargo of German-Jewish refugees had been denied admittance to Cuba.

The *Kindertransports,* as these shipments of Jewish children were called, were a remarkable—though limited—success. The story of the SS *St. Louis,* unfortunately, was more typical of the difficulties Jews faced in escaping from Nazi Germany. Nine hundred Jews, most of whom had permission to enter the United States in several years' time, reached an agreement with the Cuban government to let them live in Cuba while they waited to enter the United States. The Cuban government changed its policy just before their ship, the *St. Louis,* was due to sail in May 1939, but it sailed anyway because the passengers were desperate to get away from Germany. Cuba refused to allow the ship to dock, and the United States refused to let the passengers in ahead of schedule. The ship was finally recalled to Germany by its owners, and the sympathetic German captain, aware of what awaited his Jewish passengers back in Germany, threatened to run the ship aground on the British coast in the hope that the Jews would be rescued there. Eventually, Britain, France, Belgium, and the Netherlands agreed to take the passengers until they were able to enter the United States.

Leaving Home

"When I was at last allowed to board the train, I rushed to the window to look for my parents. I waved timidly, but even that was too much. A man in a black uniform rushed towards me, 'You Jewish swine—one more sign or word from you and we shall keep you here.'

"And so I stood at the window of the train. In the distance stood a silent and aging couple, to whom I dared neither speak nor wave a last farewell. Standing there, I was suddenly overwhelmed with a maiming certainty that I would never see my father and mother again.

"As the train pulled out of the station to wheel me to safety, I leant my face against the cold glass of the window, and wept bitterly."

Eric Lucas, one of the German-Jewish children sent to Britain on the Kindertransports, *on leaving Germany and his parents*

Unfortunately, all except those taken in by Britain were still in France, Belgium, and the Netherlands when the Germans overran those countries. Almost all of them died in the Holocaust.

Countdown to War

Time was running out. At the Munich Conference in September 1938, Hitler had promised that the transfer of the Sudetenland from Czechoslovakia to Germany would satisfy him. Just six months later, however—in March 1939—Germany occupied the rest of Czechoslovakia. This was his first outright seizure of lands—and people—that were not traditionally German. It convinced the other governments of Europe that Hitler could never be satisfied and that a European war was almost inevitable. Confirming their fears, Hitler then began demanding the return of those lands that the Treaty of Versailles had transferred from Germany to Poland. In response, the British and French told him that they would support Poland if he attacked it.

Trapped

In August 1939, Hitler and the Soviet leader, Joseph Stalin, signed an agreement—the Nazi-Soviet Pact (also known as the Hitler-Stalin Pact)—to divide up Poland between them. Stalin's aim was to buy time for the Soviets to build up their own military forces. Hitler's aim was to make sure that he did not have to fight Britain, France, and the Soviet Union at the same time. Having achieved this, he invaded Poland on September 1, 1939, and set World War II in motion.

What did this mean for Germany's Jews? In a speech in January 1939, Hitler had said that "if the international Jewish financiers in and outside Europe should succeed in plunging the nations once more into a World War," the result would be "the annihilation of the Jewish race in Europe." Did he mean it literally? The Jews now had no option but to wait and see. The outbreak of war closed the borders of Europe and made further emigration impossible. They were now trapped, and they were at Hitler's mercy.

German tanks rolled into Poland on September 1, 1939. World War II was underway, and there was now no escape for Europe's Jews.

Time Line

1914–1918 World War I.

1917 British Foreign Secretary supports idea of a Jewish homeland in Palestine.

1919 Treaty of Versailles and Treaty of St. Germain are concluded.

1923 Publication *Der Stürmer* is established by the Nazis.

1929 Great Depression begins.

1932 Nazi Party wins more seats in government than any other party in national elections in Germany.

1933 January: Adolf Hitler is appointed chancellor of Germany.
April 1: Official boycott of Jewish shops in Germany.
April: Jewish government employees are dismissed; Robert Weltsch urges Jews to take pride in themselves.
May: Books written by Jews are burned.
July: Law for the Prevention of Offspring with Hereditary Diseases is introduced.
August: Nazi government and Zionist leadership make Ha'avara Agreement.
October: Jews are dismissed from jobs in the media.

1935 May: Defense Law makes Jews ineligible for military service.
September: Nuremberg Laws come into operation, stripping Jews of their citizenship.
November: National Law of Citizenship defines "Jewishness."

1936 Summer Olympic Games are held in Berlin.

1937 "Aryanization" of Jewish businesses is accelerated.

1938 March: *Anschluss* unites Germany and Austria.
July: Evian Conference on Jewish emigration is held.
August: Evian Conference Committee tells Germany it can do what it wishes in its own country.
September: Munich Conference agrees to transfer of Czech Sudetenland to Germany.
October: Germany attempts to expel all Polish Jews.
November 7: Ernst vom Rath is shot in Paris; dies November 9.
November 9: *Kristallnacht*: Thousands of Jewish shops and synagogues are burned and destroyed, about 100 Jews are killed and 30,000 arrested (1,000 of those arrested are later killed in captivity).
November: British government decides to take in 10,000 German-Jewish children in the *Kindertransports* program.

1939 March: Germany annexes Czechoslovakia.
May: Voyage of the SS *St. Louis*.
August: Nazi-Soviet Pact is reached between Hitler and Joseph Stalin.
September 1: German attack on Poland begins World War II.

Glossary

allies: people, groups, or nations that agree to support and defend each other. "The Allies" were the nations that fought together against Germany in World War I and World War II.

anti-Semitism: prejudice against Jews.

boycott: refusal to do business or have any dealings with a particular company or other institution.

chancellor: executive head of the German government.

charity organization: group, often staffed by volunteers, that exists to help those in need.

citizen: someone having citizenship.

citizenship: rights, duties, and privileges associated with officially belonging to a country.

civilian: person who is not serving in the military.

communist: person who believes in the principles of communism, a political system in which government owns and runs the nation's economy. (A Communist with a capital "C" is a member of the Communist Party.)

concentration camp: prison camp set up by the Nazis to hold Jews and other victims of the Nazi regime. Many prisoners held in these camps were never tried or given a date of release.

democratic: based on a government system in which people vote on decisions or elect representatives to vote for them.

economic sanctions: official refusal to trade with another nation, either in particular products or in all products, in order to punish that nation or persuade it to change.

emigration: leaving of a country of residence to go and live somewhere else.

extermination camp: place set up by Nazis in which they murdered large numbers of people.

Gestapo: political police force of the Nazis.

ghetto: usually poor and overcrowded part of a city, occupied by a minority group because of social, legal, or economic pressure.

Great Depression: period of world-wide economic hardship that began in late 1929 and lasted through most of the 1930s.

Gypsy: member of a group that includes the Roma and Sinti peoples, who live mostly in Europe. Gypsies are traditionally nomadic, meaning they move from place to place.

homosexual: person attracted to others of the same sex.

immigrant: person who comes to a new country or region to take up residence.

integration: bringing or mixing together of people to break down social barriers.

Judaism: religious culture of the Jewish people that centers around a belief in a single, divine intelligence.

labor camp: camp in which prisoners are forced to perform hard labor.

Middle Ages: period of European history from about A.D. 500 to 1500.

propaganda: promotion and spreading of ideas, often involving either a selective version of the truth or plain lies.

quota: assigned proportion or number allowed.

rearmament: becoming armed with weapons after a period without any weapons.

SA: short for *Sturmabteilung*, the Nazi private army also known as "the brownshirts."

sadistic: enjoying being cruel to others.

segregation: separation of one group of people from another in order to set up barriers between them.

socialist: person who believes in socialism, a set of ideas which emphasizes the needs of the community as a whole rather than the freedoms or needs of the individual.

sterilization: practice of making people unable to have children.

stormtrooper: member of the SA.

synagogue: Jewish place of worship.

terrorist: person who performs acts of violence in order to make a political point or force a change in government policy.

Third Reich: name given by the Nazis to their regime. The name means "third empire," following the First Reich (the medieval Holy Roman Empire) and the Second Reich (1870–1918).

Zionist: member of the movement to reestablish a Jewish state in the Holy Land.

Further Resources

Books

Altman, Linda Jacobs. *Hitler's Rise to Power and the Holocaust*
(The Holocaust in History). Enslow Publishers, 2003.

Downing, David. *Fascism*. Heinemann Library, 2002.

Fox, Anne L., and Eva Abraham-Podietz. *Ten Thousand Children:
True Stories Told by Children Who Escaped the Holocaust on the
Kindertransport*. Behrman House, 1998.

Kallen, Stuart A. *The Nazis Seize Power, 1933–1939: Jewish Life Before
the Holocaust*. Abdo & Daughters, 1995.

Sherrow, Victoria. *Smoke to Flame: September 1935 to December 1938*
(Holocaust). Blackbirch Press, 1998.

Web Sites

**The Holocaust: Crimes, Heroes
and Villains**
www.auschwitz.dk
Web site about those involved in
the Holocaust, with biographies,
poetry, photos, and more.

The Holocaust History Project
www.holocaust-history.org
Archive of documents, photos,
and essays on various aspects
of the Holocaust.

Holocaust Survivors
www.holocaustsurvivors.org
Interviews, photos, and sound
recordings of survivors of the
Holocaust.

**The Museum of Tolerance's
Multimedia Learning Site**
motlc.wiesenthal.org
Educational Web site of the
Simon Wiesenthal Center, a
Jewish human rights agency.

Non-Jewish Holocaust Victims
www.holocaustforgotten.com
A site dedicated to the Nazis'
five million non-Jewish victims.

**United States Holocaust
Memorial Museum**
www.ushmm.org
Personal histories, photo
archives, and museum exhibits
of the Holocaust.

About the Author

David Downing has been writing books for adults and children
about political, military, and cultural history for thirty years.
He lives in Britain.

Index